Dancing at the Harvest

SONGS BY RAY MAKEEVER

Augsburg Fortress

Minneapolis

DANCING AT THE HARVEST
Songbook
Ray Makeever

Also available:
Dancing at the Harvest Accompaniment Edition (11-10739)
Dancing at the Harvest Compact Disc (4-5595)

Editors: Martin A. Seltz, Lani Willis
Illustration: Mary Bergherr
Cover design: David Meyer
Interior design: Lani Willis

The paper used in this publication meets the minimum requirements of American
National Standard for Information Sciences—Permanence of Paper for Printed
Materials, ANSI Z329.48-1984.   ∞ ™
Printed in the USA.

11-10738   ISBN 0-8006-5593-1
02   01   00   99   98   97   1 2 3 4 5 6 7 8 9 10

Dancing at the Harvest

Contents

Introduction

Let Us Worship God

Service Music

Gathering
People of the Word, 1
Come, let us worship God, 2
Thanksgiving to the living God, 3
Make a joyful noise, 4
Oh, come, let us worship, 5
You give, O God, 6
Rise up and sing! 7
Open our lives to the Word, 8
Kyrie, 9
God of love, have mercy, 10
Kyrie eleison, 11
This is the feast, 12
Gloria in excelsis Deo, 13
Jubilate, 14

Word
Alleluia, 15
Sing praise to the Lord, 16
Everyone who calls upon the name, 17
From the fullness of God, 18

Meal
Come, bring them to the table, 19
What have we to offer? 20
Holy, holy, holy Lord, 21
Holy, holy, 22
Lamb of God (G), 23
Lamb of God (E), 24
Lamb of God, come take away, 25
Christ, have mercy on us all, 26
Come unto me, 27
Come and dine at the table, 28
Just as Jesus told us, 29
This bread that we break, 30

Sending
Now the body broken, 31
Let us enter in, 32

Listen to My Song

Settings of the Psalms
Who are we *(Psalm 8)*, 33
I will bless you, O God *(Psalm 34)*, 34
Be merciful, O God *(Psalm 51)*, 35
Hear my cry, O God *(Psalm 61)*, 36
Rest in God alone *(Psalm 62)*, 37
Let all the people praise *(Psalm 67)*, 38
Behold and tend this vine *(Psalm 80)*, 39
Dancing at the harvest *(Psalm 85)*, 40
Come with joy *(Psalm 100)*, 41
Bless the Lord *(Psalm 103)*, 42
When you send forth your Spirit
    (Psalm 104), 43
Bless us, O God *(Psalm 128)*, 44
Show me the way *(Psalm 143)*, 45
God is compassionate *(Psalm 145)*, 46
Sing unto the Lord *(Psalm 146)*, 47
Praise and exalt God *(Psalm 148)*, 48

The Word Became Flesh

Songs for the Christmas Cycle
Blessed are you, Lord, 49
Bright and Morning Star, 50
Stir up your power, 51
For all people Christ was born, 52
Jesus, child of God, 53
Holy Child, 54
There was the Word, 55
Come and see, 56

Living in the Light
Songs for the Paschal Cycle and Baptism

I will make you into a great nation, 57
All was not well, 58
Hosanna! Come and deliver, 59
Jesus, remember me, 60
Strange King, 61
Take off your shoes, 62
Awake, O sleeper! 63
Brighter than the sun, 64
Good news, alleluia! 65
Christ has been raised, 66
Baby born again, 67
In the water, 68
Walk across the water, 69
In the last days, 70
Fill us with your Spirit, 71
Spirit of the living God, 72

See the People
Songs for the Life of Faith

Community
In spirit and truth, 73
Bring the children, 74
Open the door, 75
How the days are filled, 76
Many colors, many kinds, 77
Put on love, 78

Prayer
God we bless, 79
We can pray, 80
Instruments of your peace, 81
O loving God, 82

Justice
Holy One, in you alone, 83
We come to the hungry feast, 84
Even the stones will cry out, 85
Blessed are you, 86
On earth as in heaven, 87
Jubilee! 88
It won't be long, 89
Let peace fill the earth, 90

Commitment
Write your law upon our hearts, 91
We will serve God, 92
Around the great commandment, 93
Someone in need of your love, 94
With all your heart, 95
Give it away, 96
Tell what God has done for us, 97
Keep the faith, 98

At the Harvest
Living thanksgiving, 99
When you call, 100
Comes a new song, 101
Death be never last, 102
Between the times, 103
For to this end, 104

Indexes
Scriptural Index, 125
Alphabetical Index, 127

Introduction to Dancing at the Harvest

Making music was valued in my family. My father was a high school band director, and he and my mother sang in the church choir. I learned to play the flute and took a lot of teasing about it. Hymn singing always felt good to me. In college the sciences replaced music; I did, however, play in the Luther concert band for three years, and my senior year I bought a guitar. At seminary I set my flute aside to study theology, and sang Peter, Paul and Mary songs to relax. During my first call I realized how much I missed making music, and decided to give that some attention.

When I left pastoral ministry to take up folksinging in my mid-thirties, I had no idea that writing songs for worship would become a vocation. For a few years my immersion in the contemporary folk scene led me away from much association with the church's institutions. But my religious roots ran deep, and, eventually, they brought forth new growth in the soil of congregational life.

I came back into the church singing, and it didn't take me long to see that my sojourn outside of the church had been more of a pilgrimage than an escape. While introducing songs I had heard in the folk community, I started writing some of my own based on biblical texts and Christian themes as they came up during the seasonal cycle of the church year. These folk-style songs, with their emphasis on story and message, repetition of simple phrases, and sing-along refrains, seemed to aid both comprehension and participation in worship. My fellow members at Our Saviour's encouraged me to keep on composing. They offered me a small office in the basement and fondly referred to me as their resident Bach. Together we harvested my first hand-printed book of songs in 1984.

Thirteen years later I am still a folksinger in the church, happiest when I am standing up with my guitar before a group of people who really want to sing, who love to hear each other sing, and whose spirits are nourished as they make music together about God's presence in their lives and in their hopes for a just and peaceful world. I imagine you are one of these people.

Dancing at the Harvest is a collection of some of the songs I have most enjoyed writing, singing and leading in church settings. I am grateful to Augsburg Fortress for their willingness to publish this music and to Martin Seltz, editor, who has been my companion in organizing and compiling this work.

Countless people have encouraged and made music with me over the years, and I am thankful for you all. If I were to mention one name I would feel compelled to list everyone. Please know that if we have ever sung together in a concert, in a worship service, around a campfire, in a Sunday school room, at a convention, in a living room, in a church basement, or on a back porch, I celebrate you as part of this harvest. And I thank God for your musical friendship.

This book is dedicated to the members of Our Saviour's Lutheran Church in Minneapolis who provided the garden and much care for my first plantings.

Ray Makeever
May 1997

People of the Word

1 Peo-ple of the word: O-pen up your door   and wel-come in   the strang-er.
2 Peo-ple of the truth: O-pen up your mouth and tell   the pres-ent dan-ger.
3 Peo-ple of the heart: O-pen up your love   and re-con-cile your an-ger.
4 Peo-ple of the cross: O-pen up your arms and dance a-round the man-ger.

Peo-ple of the word: O-pen up your door   and wel-come in   the strang-er.
Peo-ple of the truth: O-pen up your mouth and tell   the pres-ent dan-ger.
Peo-ple of the heart: O-pen up your love   and re-con-cile your an-ger.
Peo-ple of the cross: O-pen up your arms and dance a-round the man-ger.

Here ev-'ry-bod-y is   wel-come all the time.   Here ev-'ry-bod-y is ac-
Not ev-'ry-bod-y is   wel-come all the time.   Not ev-'ry-bod-y is ac-
So ev-'ry-bod-y is   wel-come all the time.   So ev-'ry-bod-y is ac-
Now ev-'ry-bod-y is   wel-come all the time.   Now ev-'ry-bod-y is ac-

cept-ed   as they are.   Here ev-'ry-bod-y is   greet-ed   with a smile.
cept-ed   as they are.   Not ev-'ry-bod-y is   greet-ed   with a smile.
cept-ed   as they are.   So ev-'ry-bod-y is   greet-ed   with a smile.
cept-ed   as they are.   Now ev-'ry-bod-y is   greet-ed   with a smile.

Here ev-'ry-bod-y   is   wel-come all the time.
Not ev-'ry-bod-y   is   wel-come all the time.
So   ev-'ry-bod-y   is   wel-come all the time.
Now ev-'ry-bod-y   is   wel-come all the time.

Come, Let Us Worship God

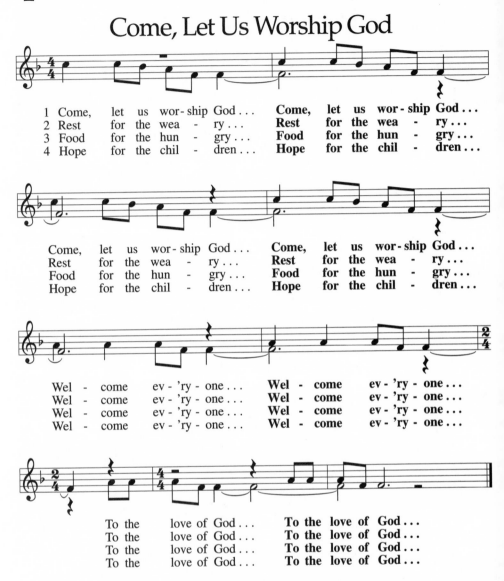

1 Come, let us wor-ship God... Come, let us wor-ship God...
2 Rest for the wea - ry... Rest for the wea - ry...
3 Food for the hun - gry... Food for the hun - gry...
4 Hope for the chil - dren... Hope for the chil - dren...

Come, let us wor-ship God... Come, let us wor-ship God...
Rest for the wea - ry... Rest for the wea - ry...
Food for the hun - gry... Food for the hun - gry...
Hope for the chil - dren... Hope for the chil - dren...

Wel - come ev -'ry - one... Wel - come ev -'ry - one...
Wel - come ev -'ry - one... Wel - come ev -'ry - one...
Wel - come ev -'ry - one... Wel - come ev -'ry - one...
Wel - come ev -'ry - one... Wel - come ev -'ry - one...

To the love of God... To the love of God...
To the love of God... To the love of God...
To the love of God... To the love of God...
To the love of God... To the love of God...

Thanksgiving to the Living God

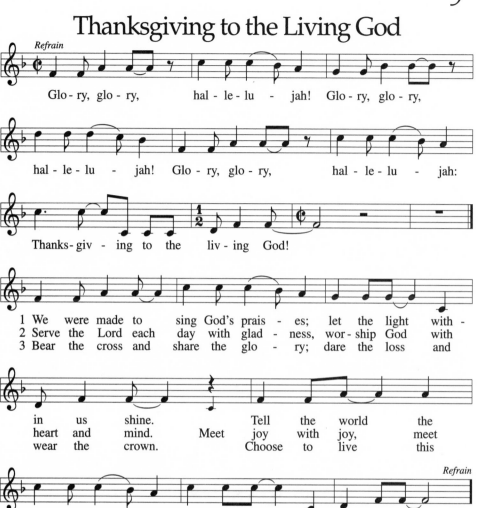

Refrain

Glo - ry, glo - ry, hal - le - lu - jah! Glo - ry, glo - ry,

hal - le - lu - jah! Glo - ry, glo - ry, hal - le - lu - jah:

Thanks- giv - ing to the liv - ing God!

1 We were made to sing God's prais - es; let the light with -
2 Serve the Lord each day with glad - ness, wor - ship God with
3 Bear the cross and share the glo - ry; dare the loss and

in us shine. Tell the world the
heart and mind. Meet joy with joy, meet
wear the crown. Choose to live this

Refrain

Lord of days is Lord of night and all of time.
sad with sad - ness, sing - ing prais - es all the time.
gos - pel sto - ry: Lose your - self and you'll be found.

4

Make a Joyful Noise

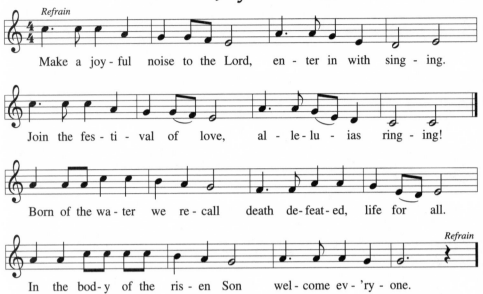

Make a joy-ful noise to the Lord, en-ter in with sing-ing.

Join the fes-ti-val of love, al-le-lu-ias ring-ing!

Born of the wa-ter we re-call death de-feat-ed, life for all.

In the bod-y of the ris-en Son wel-come ev-'ry-one.

5

Oh, Come, Let Us Worship

1 Oh, come, let us wor-ship our God. Oh, come, let us sing to our
2 Oh, come, let us wor-ship our God. Oh, come, let us sing to our
3 Oh, come, let us wor-ship our God. Oh, come, let us sing to our

God. Let us shout for joy to the Rock of our sal-va-tion:
God. Let us shout for joy to the Moth-er of cre-a-tion:
God. Let us shout for joy to the Hope of ev-'ry na-tion:

Oh, come, let us wor-ship our God.

You Give, O God

Rise Up and Sing!

Open Our Lives to the Word

1 May our words, may our songs, may our wor-ship this night
2 May our griefs, may our woes, may the sor-rows we share
3 May our joys, may our smiles, may the gifts that we bring

fill up our hearts and give us new sight. May our prayers, may our
fill up our hearts and call forth our care. May our tears, may our
fill up our hearts and stir us to sing. May we serve, may we

praise give us light for our days, and o-pen our lives to the Word.
fears be ac-cept-ed right here, and o-pen our lives to the Word.
dance, may we all take that chance; and o-pen our lives to the Word.

O - pen our lives to the liv - ing Word.
O - pen our lives to the liv - ing Word.
O - pen our lives to the liv - ing Word.

O - pen our hearts to the truth we have heard.
O - pen our hearts to the truth we have heard.
O - pen our hearts to the truth we have heard.

May our words, may our songs, may our wor-ship this night
May our griefs, may our woes, may the sor-rows we share
May our joys, may our smiles, may the gifts that we bring

o - pen our lives to the Word.
o - pen our lives to the Word.
o - pen our lives to the Word.

Kyrie

In peace, let us pray to the Lord. **Lord, have mer - cy.**

For the peace from a- bove, let us pray to the Lord. **Lord, have mer - cy.**

For the peace of the whole world, for the well - be - ing

of the church of God, for the u - ni - ty of all, let us

pray to the Lord. **Lord, have mer - cy.**

For this ho- ly house, and for all who of- fer here their wor- ship and

praise, let us pray to the Lord. **Lord, have mer - cy.**

Help, save, com- fort, and de- fend us, gra- cious Lord. **A - men**

God of Love, Have Mercy

Let us pray to God with peace in our hearts: **God of love, have mer - cy.**

For the peace from a- bove, let us pray to our God: **God of love, have mer - cy.**

For the peace of the world, for the health of the church, for the

u - ni - ty of all peo - ple, pray to our God:

God of love, have mer-cy. **God of love, have mer-cy.**

For the peo - ple of God, and for all who of - fer here their wor - ship and

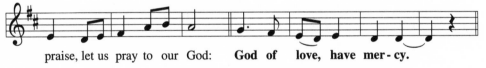

praise, let us pray to our God: **God of love, have mer - cy.**

Help, save, com-fort, and de-fend us, gra - cious God. **A - men**

Kyrie eleison

This Is the Feast

Refrain

Al- le- lu- ia, al - le- lu- ia. This is the feast of vic- t'ry

for our God. Al - le - lu - ia, al - le - lu - ia.

This is the feast, al - le - lu - ia.

1 Wor - thy is Christ, the Lamb who was slain, whose blood set us

free to be peo- ple of God. Pow- er and rich- es, wis- dom and

strength, and hon - or and bless - ing and glo - ry are his.

Refrain

Al- le- lu- ia, al - le- lu- ia. This is the feast of vic- t'ry

for our God. Al - le - lu - ia, al - le - lu - ia.

This is the feast, al - le - lu - ia.

2 Sing with all the peo - ple of God and join in the

13

Gloria in excelsis Deo

Glo-ri-a, glo-ri-a, glo - ri - a. Glo-ri-a,

glo - ri - a, glo - ri - a.

Glo - ria in ex - cel - sis De - o, in ex -

cel - sis glo - ri - a. De-

o, De - o, De - o, De - o, De - o in

ex - cel - sis glo - ri - a.

Text: traditional
Music copyright © 1983 Ray Makeever, admin. Augsburg Fortress. All rights reserved.

Jubilate

Ju - bi - la - te,   ju - bi - la - te,   ju - bi - la - te De - o.

Ju - bi - la - te,   ju - bi - la - te,   ju - bi - la - te De - o.

Ju - bi - la - te,   ju - bi - la - te,   ju - bi - la - te De - o.

Ju - bi - la - te,   ju - bi - la - te,   ju - bi - la - te

De - o.   Ju - bi - la - te,   ju - bi - la -

te,   ju - bi - la - te   De - o.

Alleluia

Al - le-lu - ia, al-le-lu - ia. Al - le-lu - ia, al - le - lu - ia.

Al - le-lu - ia, al-le-lu - ia. Al - le-lu - ia, al-le - lu - ia.

* May be sung in canon

Text: traditional

16

Sing Praise to the Lord

Sing praise to the Lord: Al - le - lu - ia,

al - le - lu - ia, our thanks be to God.

Sing praise to the Lord: Al - le - lu - ia,

al - le - lu - ia. Thanks be to God.

Everyone Who Calls Upon the Name

From the Fullness of God

From the full - ness of God have we

all re - ceived: Grace up - on grace, peace up - on peace.

From the full - ness of God have we all re - ceived:

Grace up - on grace, peace up - on peace.

Text: John 1:16, adapt.
Text and music copyright © 1983 Ray Makeever, admin. Augsburg Fortress. All rights reserved.

Come, Bring Them to the Table

Leader
Come, bring them to the ta - ble— bring the

gifts of bread and wine, the hopes and dreams of all the

peo - ple, the of - f'ring of our lives.

All
Come, bring them to the ta - ble— bring the gifts of bread and

wine, the hopes and dreams of all the peo - ple, the

of - f'ring of our lives, the of - f'ring of our lives.

What Have We to Offer?

1 What have we to of-fer?   What have we to share?
2 What have we to of-fer?   What have we to bring?
3 What have we to of-fer?   What have we to give?

Coins .. from the cof-fer,   hearts ... filled with care.
Love, .. ripe with laugh-ter;   hope that we can sing;
Eyes that are wide o-pen;   lies that we won't live;

God...... will not fal-ter;   so..... let us dare
dreams of what we're af-ter;   prom-is-es of when.
truth that must be spo-ken;   jus-tice some-how.

lay it at the al-tar   there.
Lay it at the al-tar   then.
Lay it at the al-tar   now.

(Last time only)

What have we to of-fer?   What have we to give?

Lives we will live.

Holy, Holy, Holy Lord

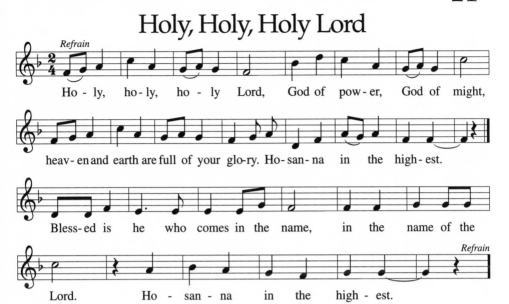

Ho - ly, ho - ly, ho - ly Lord, God of pow - er, God of might,

heav- en and earth are full of your glo-ry. Ho- san - na in the high- est.

Bless- ed is he who comes in the name, in the name of the

Lord. Ho - san - na in the high - est.

Text: International Consultation on English Texts (ICET), 1970.
Music copyright © 1983 Ray Makeever, admin. Augsburg Fortress. All rights reserved.

Holy, Holy

22

Ho-ly, ho-ly, ho-ly God, source of pow -er, source of love:

Heav-en and earth are full of you. Ho - san- na in the high - est.

Bless- ed is the one, the one who comes in the name of our gra-cious God.

Bless- ed is the one, the one who comes: Bless- ed be Je- sus Christ.

Text: traditional, adapt. Ray Makeever.
Text and music copyright © 1983 Ray Makeever, admin. Augsburg Fortress. All rights reserved.

23

Lamb of God

Lamb of God, you take a-way the sin of the world; have mer-cy on us. Lamb of God, you take a-way the sin of the world; have mer-cy on us. Lamb of God, you take a-way the sin of the world; grant us your peace, grant us your peace.

Text: traditional

24

Lamb of God

Lamb of God, you take a-way the sin of the world; have mer-cy on us. Lamb of God, you take a-way the sin of the world; have mer-cy on us. Lamb of God, you take a-way the sin of the world; grant us peace, grant us your peace.

Text: traditional

Lamb of God, Come Take Away

1 Lamb of God, come take a - way the sin of all the
2 Lamb of God, who'd give your soul to see a bro - ken
3 Lamb of God, ris - en Lord, heal us with your
4 Lamb of God, Ho - ly One, bring us peace when

world to - day: Have mer - cy up - on us, mer - cy up -
world made whole: Have mer - cy up - on us, mer - cy up -
liv - ing word: Have mer - cy up - on us, mer - cy up -
day is done: Have mer - cy up - on us, mer - cy up -

on us, mer - cy up - on us, and give us your peace.
on us, mer - cy up - on us, and give us your peace.
on us, mer - cy up - on us, and give us your peace.
on us, mer - cy up - on us, and give us your peace.

Christ, Have Mercy on Us All

1 Christ, have mer-cy on us all. Keep us stead-fast e'er we fall.
2 God, be with us at the feast. Grant us wis-dom, give us peace.
3 Ho - ly Spir-it, breathe a - gain. Light the dark-ness, be our friend.

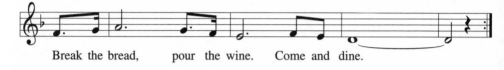

Break the bread, pour the wine. Come and dine.

4 Bake a great loaf; give it time; choose the best grapes from the vine.

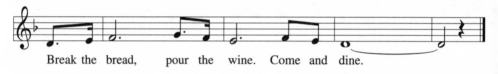

Break the bread, pour the wine. Come and dine.

27

Come unto Me

Come un-to me, all ye who la - bor; come un-to

me and I will give you rest. For my yoke, it is eas-y, and my

bur-den, it is light. Come un-to me and rest.

Text: Matt. 11:28-30, adapt.

Come and Dine at the Table

Refrain

Come and dine at the ta - ble. Drink the wine at the ta - ble.

Eat the bread at the ta - ble of the Lord.

Come and dine at the ta - ble. Drink the wine at the ta - ble.

Eat the bread at the ta - ble of the Lord.

1 On the night be - fore he died, Lord Je - sus took some friends a - side,
2 Af - ter all the friends had dined, Lord Je - sus poured a cup of wine;

then he told them he would have to go a - way.
giv - ing thanks . . . . he shared the peace and then—

As they sat a - round the ta - ble, read - y, will - ing, strong, and a - ble,
Well, he said he'd have to die, . . . and when they asked him why, . .

Refrain

Je - sus broke the bread and then was heard to say:
Je - sus passed the cup and told them once a - gain:

Just As Jesus Told Us

1 Just as Je - sus told us,   we will break this bread.
2 Just as Je - sus told us,   we will pour this wine.
3 Just as Je - sus told us,   pass the bread a - round.

Just as Je - sus told us,   we shall all be fed;
Just as Je - sus told us,   we will come and dine;
Just as Je - sus told us,   more wine can be found;

and we will re - mem - ber   what he did and said, and
and we will re - mem - ber   how he lived in time, and
and we do re - mem - ber—   bread and wine a - bound. So

how he goes on liv - ing in the bread.
how he goes on liv - ing in the wine.
break the loaf and pass the cup a - round.

This Bread That We Break

1 This bread that we break   This wine that we pour
2 This love in our heart   This faith in our mind
3 This meal that we eat   This song that we sing

Sign of the cov - e - nant re - stored:
Nour - ish the hopes of hu - man - kind:
Share we with ev - 'ry liv - ing thing:

Bod - y and blood of Christ the Lord.
Bod - y and blood for this de - signed.
Bod - y and blood to life we bring.

Now the Body Broken

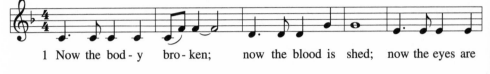

1 Now the bod-y bro-ken; now the blood is shed; now the eyes are

o-pen to the liv-ing Bread: Bread of life, Bread of hope, Bread of peace.

2 Now with wills u-nit-ed, now with o-pen hands, now with hearts de-

light-ed hear our God's com-mand: "Share the life, share the hope; share the

life, share the hope; share the life, share the hope, share the peace."

Let Us Enter In

1 Let us en-ter in to the song of thanks-giv-ing and free-dom.
2 Let us en-ter in to the place where our God has pre-ced-ed.
3 Let us en-ter in to the heart of a world that is bro-ken.

Let us en-ter in to the long line of peo-ple in need.
Let us en-ter in to the face of the fear and the pain.
Let us en-ter in to the start of a hope we can share.

Let us en-ter in to the strong mind that God is still liv-ing.
Let us en-ter in to the grace of the love when it's need-ed.
Let us en-ter in to the part where we call one an-oth-er

Heal-ing, for-giv-ing— Let us en-ter in.
Death is de-feat-ed! Let us en-ter in.
sis-ter and broth-er. Let us en-ter in.

33

Who Are We
Psalm 8

Refrain

Who are we,   that you would love us?   Who are we,   that you would

hold   us   in   your hand?   Who   are   we,   that   you   would

Last time to Coda ⊕

make us for each oth-er,   to love and hold and try   to un-der-stand?

1 Who   are   we   be-neath the   hea-vens,   'neath the
2 Who   are   we   a-mong the   crea-tures?   Some that

stars   and   all   the   mys-ter-ies   a-far?   Who   are
crawl,   some wing-ing   swift-ly through the sky,   some that

we   up-on   an   earth   so rich for   grow-ing?
swim,   and some that   walk   up-on their   two   feet—

Refrain

Can   you   tell   us   who   we real-ly   are?
Who   are   we   and   can   you tell   us   why?

Listen to My Song

Coda

(Thanks be to God)

stand.   Bless   the   Lord—   that you would

(Thanks be to God)

love us!   Bless   the   Lord—   that you would

(Thanks be to God)

hold us   in your hand! Bless the   Lord—   that you would

make us for each oth - er,   to   love and hold and try   to un - der -

stand.   Let us   bless the Lord: Thanks be   to   God.

34

I Will Bless You, O God
Psalm 34

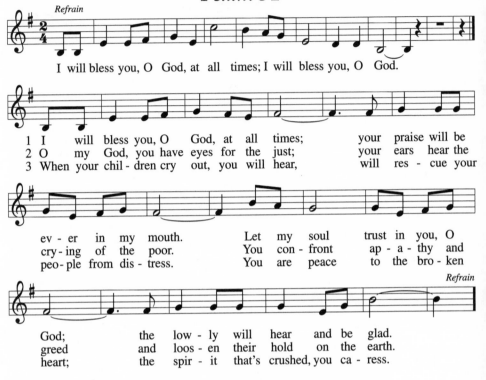

Refrain

I will bless you, O God, at all times; I will bless you, O God.

1 I will bless you, O God, at all times; your praise will be
2 O my God, you have eyes for the just; your ears hear the
3 When your chil-dren cry out, you will hear, will res - cue your

ev - er in my mouth. Let my soul trust in you, O
cry-ing of the poor. You con - front ap - a - thy and
peo-ple from dis - tress. You are peace to the bro - ken

Refrain

God; the low - ly will hear and be glad.
greed and loos - en their hold on the earth.
heart; the spir - it that's crushed, you ca - ress.

Be Merciful, O God
Psalm 51

Be mer-ci-ful, O God, for we have sinned.

1 Have mer-cy on me, God, in your good-ness; in the
2 For I con-fess to you my of-fens-es; and my

great-ness of your love make me clean with-in......
sin is al-ways there keep-ing me from right. A-

Wash me from my guilt and cleanse me from my sin.
gainst you I have sinned, done e-vil in your sight.

3 O God, cre-ate in me .. a .... clean heart and re-
4 Oh, give me back the joy of your sal-va-tion, and sus-

new a stead-fast spir-it deep with-in my be-ing.
tain a will-ing spir-it in me all my days. ...

Cast me not a-way; take not your spir-it from me.
O-pen now my lips; I shall de-clare your praise. . .

Hear My Cry, O God
Psalm 61

Hear my cry, O God; lis-ten to my prayer. Lis-ten to my song:

Sing-ing prais-es all a-long. 1 I

(1) call on you a - gain, for you have called me
2 With a wear - y heart, I feel so far a -
3 Hold me in your arms; . . . . . shel - ter me from
4 Hear a - gain my vow: . . . . . . I will serve you

friend, you have called me friend; so I
part, feel so far a - part, with a
harm, shel - ter me from harm; hold me,
now, I will serve you now. Hear a -

Refrain

call on you once a - gain.
wear - y, wear - y heart.
hold . . . . me in your arms.
gain, ... Lord, hear my vow.

Listen to My Song

Harmony

Hear my cry, O God; lis-ten to my prayer. Lis-ten to my song:

Sing-ing prais-es all a - long. 1 I

(1) call on you a - gain, for you have called me friend,
2 With a wear - y heart, I feel so far a - part,
3 Hold me in your arms; . . . . . shel - ter me from harm,
4 Hear a - gain my vow: . . . . . I will serve you now,

you have called me friend; so I call on you once a - gain.
feel so far a - part, with a wear - y, wear - y heart.
shel - ter me from harm; hold me, hold . . . me in your arms.
I will serve you now. Hear a - gain, . . . Lord, hear my vow.

37

Rest in God Alone
Psalm 62

Refrain

Rest in God a - lone, my soul; oh, rest in God, my soul.

Rest in God a - lone, my soul; oh, rest in God, my soul.

1 On - ly in God is my soul at rest. . . . . . From
2 On - ly in God be at rest, my soul; . . . . . from
3 God is my safe - ty and God my glo - ry. God

God comes my sal - va - tion. God on - ly is my
God comes hope for each day. God on - ly is my
is the source of my strength. Trust God in ev - 'ry

Refrain

rock, my strong - hold. I shall not be dis - turbed.
rock, my strong - hold, the love for ev - 'ry way.
time, O peo - ple; pour out your hearts to God.

Let All the People Praise
Psalm 67

Refrain

Let all the peo - ple praise you, God. Let all the peo-

Optional handclaps

ple praise you, God.

1 Bless us, O God, show us your kind - ness, and
2 All the earth shall fol - low your ways, O God,
3 Let all peo - ple joy - ful - ly sing this song:
4 God has blessed us, giv - en us sun and rain.
5 May our God con - tin - ue to bless us, and

Refrain

make your face to shine . . . up - on us and—
na - tions know your pow - er to save, O God.
God is bring - ing jus - tice and right - ing wrong.
Earth has yield - ed bush - els of fruit and grain.
may the whole earth sing out a loud a - men.

Behold and Tend This Vine
Psalm 80

Look down from heav-en, O God; be - hold and tend this vine.

Look down from heav-en, O God; be-hold and tend this vine.

Text: Ps. 80:7-14; Book of Common Prayer, 1979.
Music copyright © 1997 Ray Makeever, admin. Augsburg Fortress. All rights reserved.

7 Restore us, O | God of hosts;*
show the light of your countenance, and we | shall be saved.
8 You have brought a vine | out of Egypt;*
you cast out the nations and | planted it.
Refrain

9 You prepared the | ground for it;*
it took root and | filled the land.
10 The mountains were covered | by its shadow*
and the towering cedar trees | by its boughs.
Refrain

11 You stretched out its tendrils | to the sea*
and its branches | to the river.
12 Why have you broken | down its wall,*
so that all who pass by pluck | off its grapes?
Refrain

13 The wild boar of the forest has | ravaged it,*
and the beasts of the field have | grazed upon it.
14 Turn now, O God of hosts, look down from heaven;
behold and | tend this vine;*
preserve what your right | hand has planted.
Refrain

Dancing at the Harvest
Psalm 85

Refrain

Lord, Lord, Lord, let us see your kind - ness.

Lord, Lord, Lord, grant us your sal - va - tion.

1 I will hear what God pro - claims God pro - claims
2 Truth and kind - ness now shall meet now shall meet
3 God will give us ben - e - fits ben - e - fits

Peace .. to the peo - ple Peace .. to the peo - ple
Peace .. kiss - ing jus - tice Peace .. kiss - ing jus - tice
Danc - ing at the har - vest Danc - ing at the har - vest

Come to those who fear your name fear your name
Truth shall spring out from the earth from the earth
Jus - tice now will lead the way lead the way

Refrain

Glo - ry dwell - ing in our land Glo - ry dwell - ing in our land.
Jus - tice rain from heav - en Jus - tice rain from heav - en.
Foot - prints of sal - va - tion Foot - prints of sal - va - tion.

Come with Joy
Psalm 100

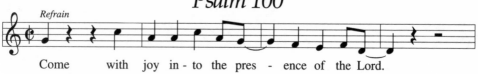

Come with joy in-to the pres - ence of the Lord.

Come with joy in-to the pres - ence of the Lord.

1 Sing joy-ful-ly to the Lord, all you lands; serve the Lord

with glad-ness. Come be-fore your God with joy-ful sing - ing.

2 Know that the Lord is God: God made us,

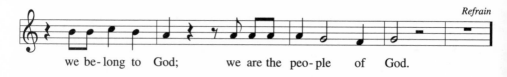

we be-long to God; we are the peo-ple of God.

Listen to My Song

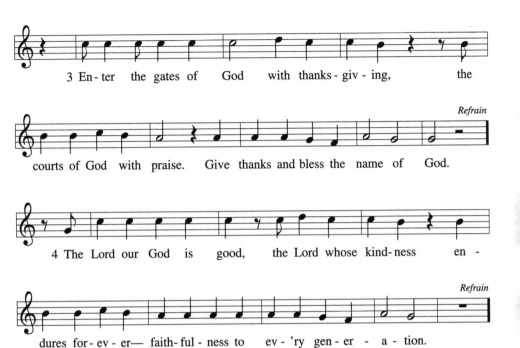

3 Enter the gates of God with thanks-giv-ing, the
courts of God with praise. Give thanks and bless the name of God. *Refrain*

4 The Lord our God is good, the Lord whose kind-ness en-
dures for-ev-er— faith-ful-ness to ev-'ry gen-er-a-tion. *Refrain*

Bless the Lord
Psalm 103

Refrain

Bless the Lord, O my soul. Oh, let all that is with-in me bless the ho- ly name of God.

1 God for - gives all of us all of our sin,
2 God gives us all of the good things of life,
3 God will not al - ways ac - cuse us of wrong
4 As high as heav - ens are a - bove the earth,

Bless the

heals us and will help us time and a - gain,
re - news our youth like the ea - gle in flight.
and will not hold on to an - ger for long,
so great God's mer - cy and all we are worth;

Lord.

Bless the

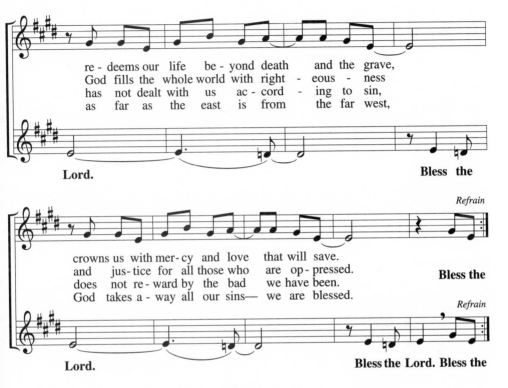

re - deems our life be - yond death and the grave,
God fills the whole world with right - eous - ness
has not dealt with us ac - cord - ing to sin,
as far as the east is from the far west,

Lord. Bless the

Refrain

crowns us with mer- cy and love that will save.
and jus- tice for all those who are op- pressed.
does not re - ward by the bad we have been.
God takes a - way all our sins— we are blessed.

Bless the

Refrain

Lord. Bless the Lord. Bless the

43

When You Send Forth Your Spirit
Psalm 104

Refrain

When you send forth your Spir - it,

we are re - newed, we are re - newed.

When you send forth your Spir - it,

last time: (𝄐)

we are re - newed, we are re - newed.

1 Man - i - fold your works, O God of might:
2 When we look to you to give us food,
3 May the glo - ry of our God en - dure.
4 Now may e - vil cease up - on the earth;

Mak - er of the earth, the air, the light.
you o - pen your hand, fill us with good.
May our God be glad, be strong, be sure.
wick - ed - ness no more shall be of worth.

Wa - ters great and wide and all there - in,
When you hide your face, we are dis - mayed;
Un - to you, O God, our praise we give:
Pleas - ing God shall be our on - ly goal.

Refrain

crea - tures that a - bide, let life be - gin.
when you take a - way our breath, we fade.
We will sing your glo - ry while we live.
Al - le - lu - ia! Bless - ed be God, my soul.

Listen to My Song

Bless Us, O God
Psalm 128

Refrain

Bless us, O God; bless us, O God; bless us all the days of our lives.
Bless us, O God; bless us, O God; bless us all the days of our lives.

1 Bless-ed are you who fear and walk the way of the liv-ing God. You shall eat the fruit of your la-bor, you shall be hap-py and fa - vored.

2 Your spouse will be like a fruit-ful vine grow-ing in your gar - den. Your chil-dren will be like ol-ive branch - es grow-ing in the sun 'round your ta-ble.

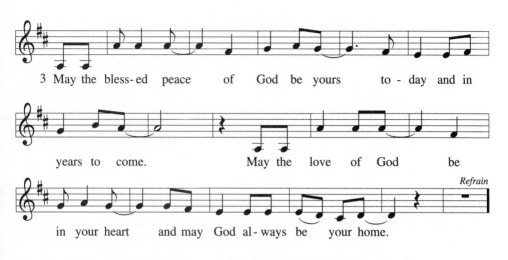

3 May the bless-ed peace of God be yours to - day and in

years to come. May the love of God be

Refrain

in your heart and may God al-ways be your home.

45

Show Me the Way
Psalm 143

1 .... Lord, ... hear .... my prayer.
2 .... Hold.... me not ..... to blame.
3 I re - call.... the works of your hands.
4 .. I spread out my hands ... to you.
5 .... Speak to my fail - ing Spir - it.
6 Let me know... your love in the morn-ing.
7 .. I lift up my soul .... to you.

Show me the way,

show me the way.

.... Lord, ... hear .... my prayer. .. O
.... Hold.... me not ..... to blame. .. O
I re - call.... the works of your hands. .. O
I spread out my hands ... to you. .... O
.... Speak to my fail - ing Spir - it. O
Let me know.... your love in the morn-ing. O
I lift up my soul .... to you. ..... O

Lord, show me the way.

God Is Compassionate
Psalm 145

Refrain:
God is com-pas-sion-ate to all crea-tures.

1 Ev - 'ry day I will bless you, O God.
2 Let all crea - tures give you thanks, O God.
3 Be to all the heal - ing core of life.

I will praise your name for - ev - er and ev - er.
Let your whole cre - a - tion bless you with sing - ing.
With the splen - dor of the u - ni - verse fill us.

Great are you and high - ly to be praised; the
We will tell the glo - ry of your works and
You are faith - ful to cre - a - tion; your

mys - t'ry of your good - ness is un - search - a - ble.
live the sto - ry of your pow - er and your love.
mer - cy flows to ev - 'ry gen - er - a - tion.

Sing unto the Lord
Psalm 146

Sing un-to the Lord, O my soul, O my soul!

Sing un-to the Lord, O my soul!

1 I will sing your prais-es as long as I live:
2 You are faith-ful ev-er, the eyes for the blind,
3 Friend un-to the strang-er, the lost and the blamed;

Refrain

I will play for you while I am breath-ing, breath-ing! breath-ing!
man-na for the hun-gry, cap-tives free-ing, free-ing! free-ing!
cour-age to a low-ly peo-ple sing-ing, sing-ing! sing-ing!

48

Praise and Exalt God
Psalm 148

Handclaps

Refrain

Sing glo - ry! and ev - er - last - ing praise to God.

Sing glo - ry! and ev - er - last - ing praise.

1 Sun and moon and stars a - bove: Sing praise and ex - al - t God for - ev-er.
2 Hail and rain and wind and snow: Sing praise and ex - al - t God for - ev-er.
3 Moun-tains lift - ing up the earth: Sing praise and ex - al - t God for - ev-er.
4 Men and wom-en, old and young: Sing praise and ex - al - t God for - ev-er.

An - gels, hosts, all praise the name: Sing praise and ex - al - t God.
Wa - ters in the earth be-low: Sing praise and ex - al - t God.
Blos-soms bring-ing fruit to birth: Sing praise and ex - al - t God.
All the na - tions, ev - 'ry tongue: Sing praise and ex - al - t God.

Plan-ets, sys - tems, gal - ax - ies: Sing praise and ex - al - t God for - ev-er.
Fire so pow-er - ful and bright: Sing praise and ex - al - t God for - ev-er.
An - i - mals both wild and tame: Sing praise and ex - al - t God for - ev-er.
Peo - ple sing this end - less song: Sing praise and ex - al - t God for - ev-er.

Refrain

U - ni - ver - sal mys - ter - ies: Sing praise and ex - al - t God.
South-ern storms and north-ern lights: Sing praise and ex - al - t God.
Creep-ing, fly - ing, walk-ing, lame: Sing praise and ex - al - t God.
Sing and sing and sing a - long: Sing praise and ex - al - t God.

Exalt *is sung with three syllables: ex-al-teh*

Blessed Are You, Lord

Blessed are you, Lord, the | God of Israel,*
you have come to your people and | set them free.
You have raised up for us a | mighty Savior,*
born of the house of your | servant David.

Through your holy prophets, you promised of old
    to save us | from our enemies,*
from the hands of | all who hate us,
to show mercy | to our forebears,*
and to remember your | holy covenant.

This was the oath you swore to our | father Abraham:*
to set us free from the hands | of our enemies,
free to worship you | without fear,*
holy and righteous before you, all the days | of our life.

And you, child, shall be called the prophet of | the Most High,*
for you will go before the Lord to pre- |pare the way,
to give God's people knowledge | of salvation*
by the forgiveness | of their sins.

In the tender compassion | of our God*
the dawn from on high shall break | upon us,
to shine on those who dwell in darkness and the sha- |dow of death,*
and to guide our feet into the | way of peace.

Glory to the Father, and | to the Son*
and to the | Holy Spirit:
as it was in the begin- |ning, is now,*
and will be forev- |er. Amen

50

Bright and Morning Star

1 In a cir-cle in the night the qui-et folk are gath-ered. In ref-uge from the world-ly fight, they're leav-ing all that's mat-tered far be-hind. In prayer-ful pose they watch the sky a - far: Wait-ing for that shin-ing rose, the Bright and Morn-ing Star.

2 The watch-ers on the high-est height stand look-ing toward the mor-row, the prom-ised end to end-less night that leaves the lone-some sor-row far be - hind. In prayer-ful pose they watch the sky a - far: Wait-ing for that shin-ing rose, the Bright and Morn-ing Star.

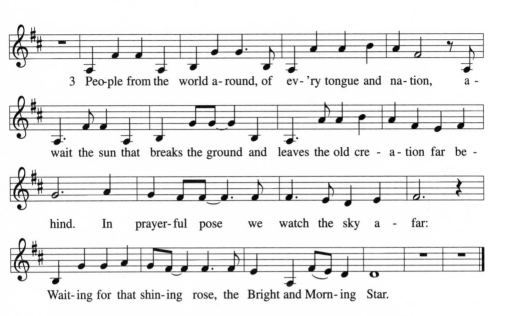

3 Peo-ple from the world a-round, of ev-'ry tongue and na-tion, a-
wait the sun that breaks the ground and leaves the old cre-a-tion far be-
hind. In prayer-ful pose we watch the sky a-far:
Wait-ing for that shin-ing rose, the Bright and Morn-ing Star.

51

Stir Up Your Power

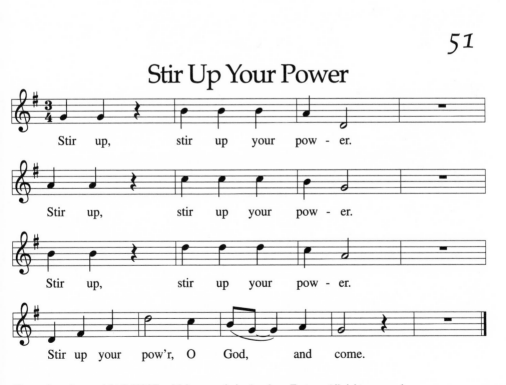

Stir up, stir up your pow - er.

Stir up, stir up your pow - er.

Stir up, stir up your pow - er.

Stir up your pow'r, O God, and come.

52

For All People Christ Was Born

1 For all peo-ple Christ was born on that qui - et Christ-mas morn:
2 For all peo-ple Christ has come down from heav'n to earth - ly home:
3 For all peo-ple Christ can be grace and truth and love set free:

Star of Dav - id, bright and warm for all.
Gift of free - dom, God a - lone for all.
Light and life for you, for me, for all.

53

Jesus, Child of God

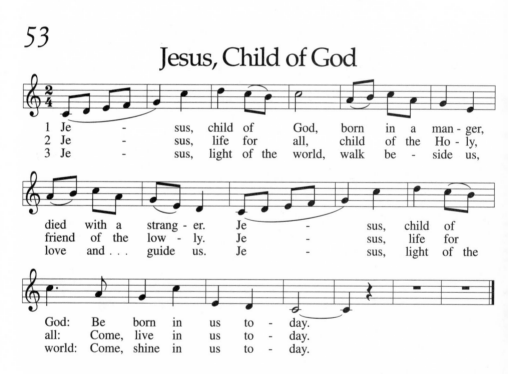

1 Je - sus, child of God, born in a man - ger,
2 Je - sus, life for all, child of the Ho - ly,
3 Je - sus, light of the world, walk be - side us,

died with a strang - er. Je - sus, child of
friend of the low - ly. Je - sus, life for
love and . . . guide us. Je - sus, light of the

God: Be born in us to - day.
all: Come, live in us to - day.
world: Come, shine in us to - day.

Holy Child

1 Strang-ers on the road from Beth - le - hem,
Dan - gers soon to come in Beth - le - hem,
2 Strang-ers on the road from E - gypt's land,
Dan - gers come and gone in Beth - le - hem—
3 Strang-ers on the road, why leave your home?
Dan - gers come and go in ev - 'ry land—

1 why do you trav - el at this mid - night hour?
blood to be shed . . in the quest for power,
2 why do you trav - el in the des - ert sun?
Blood of the in - no - cent, the ho - ly ones
3 Why do you trav - el till the break of dawn?
Blood of the in - no - cent, the Ho - ly One

1 You could be a - sleep and qui - et watch be keep-ing o'er your
bids us take the road to guard our pre - cious load, ... our
2 You could be at rest, now would-n't that be best . . . for your
bids us to re - turn, to live and love and learn . . with our
3 Why keep faith-ful watch, why pay the pain - ful cost . . . of the
bids us to the feast to break the bread of peace . . with the

1
1 child, your Ho-ly Child.
child,
2 child, your Ho-ly Child.
child,
3 child, the Ho-ly Child.
child,

2
our Ho-ly Child.
our Ho-ly Child.
the Ho-ly Child.

Refrain
Ho-ly Child, Ho-ly Child, born in the dark-ness, child of night.

Ho-ly Child, Ho-ly Child: You bear our hope, you car-ry our light.

There Was the Word

1 Be-fore there was earth or wa-ter or sky Be-fore there was

how or where or why Be-fore there was wom-an Be-

fore there was man Be-fore there was "No" and be-fore there was

"Oh, yes I can"— There was the Word.

2 Then came cre-a-tion Then came the fall Then came the flood And

then came the call Then came the prom-ise Then came the

land Then came cap-tiv-i-ty And then came the wil-der-ness

band— And there was the Word.

Refrain

And the Word be-came flesh And the Word be-came bone

And the Word be-came one of our own.

The Word Became Flesh

3 Some called him sav - ior Some called him king Some
called him the one who would change ev - 'ry - thing
Some called him truth Some called him grace Some
called him the light to en - light - en the whole hu - man
race— And there was the Word. *Refrain*

4 Wher - ev - er false - hood is turned in - to right
Wher - ev - er blind - ness is turned in - to sight
Wher - ev - er death is turned in - to birth
Wher - ev - er war - fare is turned in - to peace on this
earth— There is the Word. *Refrain*

Come and See

Refrain

We have found the Mes-si - ah— in the wa-ter.

We have found the Mes-si - ah— on the road to

Gal - i - lee found the Mes-si - ah.

Come and see, oh, come and see.

1 Well, John saw the Spir - it when the Ho - ly Dove—
2 "Be - hold," said . . . John, "the Lamb who takes a - way"—
3 When we ask . . . Je - sus, "Where . . . do you stay?"—

Come and see, oh, come and see.
Come and see, oh, come and see.
Come and see, oh, come and see.

Came down to . . . . rest . . . . on the light of love.
"The sin and the e - vil in the world to - day."
"Come, fol - low . . . . me and I will show the way."

Refrain

Come and see, oh, come and see.
Come and see, oh, come and see.
Come and see, oh, come and see.

I Will Make You into a Great Nation

Refrain

I will make you in-to a great na-tion; I will bless you in all you do, so all the peo-ple, all the peo-ple of the earth may be blessed through you. I will make you in-to a strong peo-ple; I will keep you a-long the way, so all your broth-ers and your sis-ters on the earth may be blessed through you this day.

1 So leave your coun-try, leave your home; leave the plac-es you've out-grown. Go to a new land, I'll show you where: You will know it when you're there.

2 As ev-'ry sea-son turns with time, the rhy-thms start to rhyme. So when the prom-ise be-comes the sign, you will know that you are mine.

Refrain

All Was Not Well

1 All was not well as the wom-an drew
2 All was not well as the wom-an drew
3 All was not well as the wom-an drew

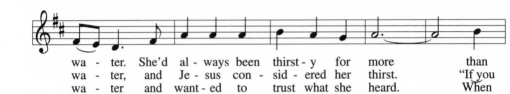

wa - ter. She'd al - ways been thirst - y for more than
wa - ter, and Je - sus con - sid - ered her thirst. "If you
wa - ter and want - ed to trust what she heard. When

she . . . . . could drink from man - y the buck - et - ful
knew who I was and what I can give you, you'd
Je - sus ex - plained and told her his name she said,

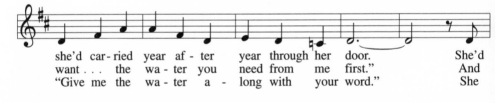

she'd car - ried year af - ter year through her door. She'd
want . . . the wa - ter you need from me first." And
"Give me the wa - ter a - long with your word." She

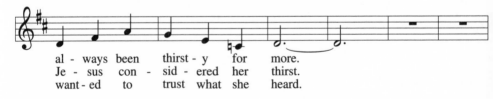

al - ways been thirst - y for more.
Je - sus con - sid - ered her thirst.
want - ed to trust what she heard.

All was not well as the wom-an drew wa - ter, and Je - sus sat
All was not well as the wom-an drew wa - ter and lis - tened to
All was not well as the wom-an drew wa - ter. So Je - sus ex -

thirst- y near - by. "Come, give me a drink of wa - ter," said
what Je- sus said. Said she, . . . "I'd glad - ly drink what you
tend- ed his hand and drew her an o - cean of life - giv - ing

he. "How can you ask it?" she said with a
of - fer, but then you and I'd both be bet - ter off
wa - ter, chang - ing the rules with this sim - ple com -

sigh, "for I'm a Sa - mar - i - tan and you are a
dead— for I am a wom - an and you are a
mand: "Though you're a Sa - mar - i - tan and I am a

Jew. You know and I know what we can - not
man. You know and I know, we both un - der -
Jew, and you know and I know what we can - not

do: This cup can - not pass be - tween me and
stand: This cup can - not pass be - tween me and
do: This cup must pass . . . . . be - tween me and

Last time to Coda ⊕

you, yet you're act - ing as if it weren't true."
you, yet you're act - ing as if it weren't true."
you, or the life we are liv - ing's not true."

Coda on next page ▶

Though "I am a wom - an" and "I am a man,"
you know and I know, we both un - der - stand:
This cup must pass be - tween me and you, or the
life we are liv - ing's not true.

Hosanna! Come and Deliver

Jesus, Remember Me

Refrain

Je-sus, re - mem - ber me, Je-sus, re - mem - ber

me when I am lost, count - in' the cost,

Je - sus, re - mem - ber me.

1 Re - mem-ber me, Je - sus, and all of your chil - dren as you're
2 Re - mem-ber me, Je - sus, and all of the peo - ple who are
3 Re - mem-ber me, Je - sus, and all who are cap - tive; come and

hang - in' up there on the tree. So beau-ti - f'lly
hang - in' a - long - side of you. The in - no - cent
set all the pris - on - ers free. Come, take off our

Refrain

born, now dy - in' in scorn: Je - sus, re - mem - ber me.
die and we don't know why: Je - sus, come, car - ry us through.
chains and re - call our names: Je - sus, re - mem - ber me.

Strange King

1 Strange King on a cross We have gained what you have lost
2 Strange King on the tree High on the mount of Cal - va - ry
3 Strange King in the tomb Dark the man - ger, still no room
4 Strange King from the grave Come a - gain your peo - ple save

Your life giv - en for us Strange King on a cross.
Your death set - ting us free Strange King on the tree.
Your death came so soon Strange King in the tomb.
Your life, all you gave Strange King from the grave.

Refrain

What a strange way to be - come a king Dy - ing on a cross

What a strange way to be - come a king Dy - ing for us.

Take Off Your Shoes

Lov-ing them to the end, Je-sus was eat-ing with his friends when he took up a towel and he start-ed to wash their feet. Si-mon Pe-ter thought this was wrong: "This is not where my Lord be-longs, here on the floor. And what's more," he said, "you nev-er will wash my feet." Know-ing that he did-n't un-der-stand, Je-sus looked straight back at this stub-born man and said, "I'll wash your feet." He said, "I'll wash your feet, I will wash your feet or you'll have no part in me." He said it gent-ly, so gent-ly.

Take off your shoes and I'll wash your feet. You can do the same

thing for me next time we meet. Take off your shoes and I'll

wash your skin, and the love of God will come pour-in' in.

63

Awake, O Sleeper!

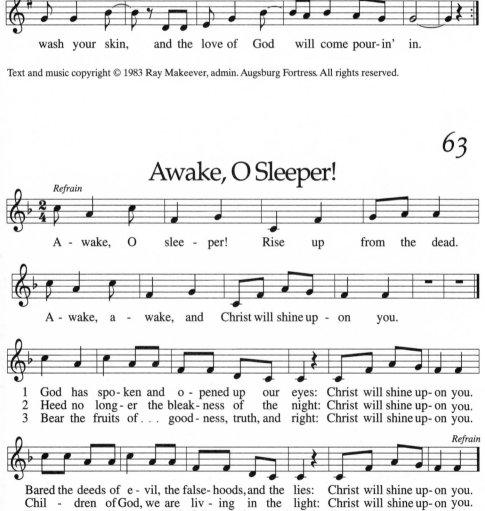

A - wake, O slee - per! Rise up from the dead.

A - wake, a - wake, and Christ will shine up - on you.

1 God has spo - ken and o - pened up our eyes: Christ will shine up-on you.
2 Heed no long - er the bleak- ness of the night: Christ will shine up-on you.
3 Bear the fruits of . . . good- ness, truth, and right: Christ will shine up-on you.

Bared the deeds of e - vil, the false- hoods, and the lies: Christ will shine up-on you.
Chil - dren of God, we are liv - ing in the light: Christ will shine up-on you.
Feast on what is ho - ly and full of hope and might: Christ will shine up-on you.

Brighter than the Sun

Refrain

Bright - er, bright-er than the sun is the can - dle of the
Ho - ly One. Big - ger, big-ger than the sea are the
waves of God wash - ing o - ver me.

1 Gon - na light my can - dle from the ho - ly flame
2 Gon - na meet God's chil - dren at the foun - tain of life,
3 Gon - na gath - er 'round and gon - na wel - come in

of the one that's bright - er than . . . my . . . own name.
where the word and the wa - ter and the Lord . . Je - sus Christ
ev - 'ry child to be and ev - 'ry one who's ev - er been.

Gon - na wash my bod - y in the ho - ly sea,
make a new cre - a - tion out of ev - 'ry one:
Gon - na breathe to - geth - er with this spark of life:

Refrain

in the wat - er of life that's . . . big - ger than me. Oh,—
Ho - ly Spir - it of love, let the wa - ters run. Oh,—
Ho - ly Spir - it of God, make our flame burn bright. Oh,—

Living in the Light

Refrain—optional harmony

Bright - er, bright- er than the sun is the can - dle of the Ho - ly One. Big - ger, big- ger than the sea are the waves of God wash - ing o - ver me.

Good News, Alleluia!

Good news, al-le-lu-ia! There's a whole lot of good news on this day. Good news, al-le-lu-ia! Well, some-one has rolled the stone a - way.

1 On the first day of the week, Mar-y Mag-da-lene went to the tomb be-fore the break of dawn. The stone had been moved and the grave was emp-ty and the bro-ken bod-y of Je - sus was gone.

2 Mar-y ran and she ran to tell Si-mon Pe-ter and the oth-er dis-ci-ple, the one named John, that the stone had been moved and the *Refrain* grave was emp-ty and the bro-ken bod-y of Je - sus was gone.

3 John out - ran Pe - ter to the tomb, looked in, and saw the clothes of Je - sus ly-ing on the ground. Pe-ter ar - rived, went in - *Refrain* side, but the bod-y of the one who had died was not to be found.

4 Then John came in, and to - geth - er they won-dered where the bro - ken bod - y of their Lord had gone. John saw and be - lieved, though he could not con - ceive of how the *Refrain* one who had died could go liv - ing on.

Christ Has Been Raised

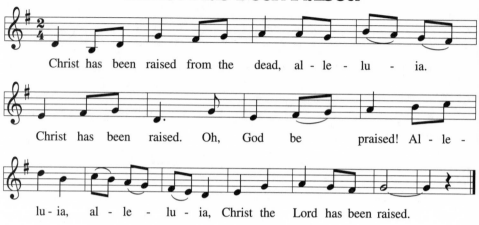

Christ has been raised from the dead, al - le - lu - ia.

Christ has been raised. Oh, God be praised! Al - le -

lu - ia, al - le - lu - ia, Christ the Lord has been raised.

Baby Born Again

1 Ba - by born, now born a - gain in the wa - ter
2 Ba - by born, this gift re - ceive. Let all e - vil
3 Ba - by born, now born a - new, let God's Spir - it

with - out end. Ba - by born, now born once more
now take leave. Ba - by born, let good im - part
dwell in you. Ba - by born, be wel - come here.

in the Word that we a - dore, the
joy and peace with - in your heart, all
Let our love dis - pel all fear, and

liv - ing Word that we a - dore.
joy and peace with - in your heart.
let our love dis - pel all fear.

Living in the Light

Harmony

1 Ba - by born, now born a - gain in the wa - ter
2 Ba - by born, this gift re - ceive. Let all e - vil
3 Ba - by born, now born a - new, let God's Spir - it

with - out end. Ba - by born, now born once more
now take leave. Ba - by born, let good im - part
dwell in you. Ba - by born, be wel - come here.

in the Word that we a - dore, the
joy and peace with - in your heart, all
Let our love dis - pel all fear, and

liv - ing Word that we a - dore.
joy and peace with - in your heart.
let our love dis - pel all fear.

68

In the Water

1 In the be - gin - ning . . . . God cre - a - ted light,
2 Build - ing an ark, No - ah did as he was told
3 "Come un - to me, lay your heav - y bur - den down;"
4 Drink from the well and your thirst will go a - way;

heav - en and the earth and hu - man - kind,
though he nev - er ful - ly rea - soned why.
rest . . . . . in the shade be - neath the tree.
there will come a day when it re - turns.

moun - tains and val - leys and fish to fill the seas: The
Af - ter the flood, well, he did - n't need to ask: His
Cool your . . . . feet at the bot - tom of the stream: It
"Drink from . . . . me and you will not thirst a - gain": For

world was born to liv - ing in the wa - ter.
task had been sur - viv - al in the wa - ter.
seems that there is heal - ing in the wa - ter.
life is nev - er end - ing in the wa - ter.

Refrain

In the wa - ter In the wa - ter In the wa - ter and the

word the voice of God is heard. In the wa - ter In the

wa - ter In the wa - ter we have been bap - tized.

Walk across the Water

1 When the wa - ters of our moth - er broke and the
2 On the day we came to be bap - tized, by the
3 And when Is - rael fled from E - gypt's land, they were
4 Is that that my Lord a - walk - ing ▬ on the

world first came to be— It was
word in the wa - ter freed, Je - sus
chased up to the sea. Mo - ses'
Sea of Gal - i - lee? Je - sus

in that in - stant God done spoke and said,
looked in - to our won - d'ring eyes and said,
God said, "Take them by the hand.... and
says, "If your faith be more than talk,..... then

"Walk a - cross the wa - ter to me."
"Walk a - cross the wa - ter to me."
walk a - cross the wa - ter to me."
walk a - cross the wa - ter to me."

Refrain

"Walk a - cross the wa - ter. Walk a - cross the

wa - ter. Let your faith run free on the rag - ing sea,

and walk a - cross the wa - ter to me."

In the Last Days

In the last days it shall be that I will pour out my Spir - it: And your sons and your daugh - ters will proph - e - sy, the young will see vi - sions, the old dream why, and the ser - vants of God will be lift - ed high— in the last days it shall be.

Text: Joel 2:28, adapt.

Fill Us with Your Spirit

Pour out on the ones you love a mea-sure of your grace, a sign of power.

Fill us with your Ho - ly Spir - it and will us at this hour to pour out on the ones you love the trea-sure of our faith; our hope re - lease. Fill us with your Spir - it, with your peace.

Spirit of the Living God

Spir-it of the liv-ing God, sur-round us with your light. Ho-ly Spir-it of the liv-ing God, breathe in and make it all right. right. Breathe in and make it all right.

Living in the Light

1 Je - sus spoke sim - ply so that all could un - der -
2 How can we live as though dark - ness is the

stand. The les - son... he taught .. us was to
king and hold - in' on to what we've got is the

give a help - ing hand: Share your food with ... the
best and high - est thing, when the one who loves us

hun - gry, cloth - ing with the poor, and love .. with your
most of all gave it all a - way, then rose up from his

Refrain

neigh - bor liv - ing right next door.
dy - ing to live .. an - oth - er day?

In Spirit and Truth

1 In spir - it and truth we come to wor - ship
2 In spir - it and truth we give our bur - dens
3 In spir - it and truth we come with thanks to
4 In spir - it and truth we gath - er at the
5 In spir - it and truth and grace that fills our

our God: Source of all liv - ing,
to God, trust - ing the prom - ise
our God, who in all kind - ness
ta - ble, shar - ing Christ's bod - y;
liv - ing we love our neigh - bors,

joy of our thanks - giv - ing, who has made us, re -
peace will come up - on us. We are crea - tures, de -
comes to us and finds us. Please pro - tect us, re -
Ho - ly Lamb of God, we know you heed us and
bless - ings from our Sav - ior. Christ, be with us and

deemed us, and leads us with a love that frees us—
fense - less, we sense in Christ a life that's end - less.
spect us, and with your gen - tle touch ca - ress us.
feed us to do the same for those who need us.
guide us, a - bide with us your faith - ful ser - vants,

Je - sus, in spir - it and truth.
Mend us in spir - it and truth.
Bless us in spir - it and truth.
Lead us in spir - it and truth.
fer - vent in spir - it and truth.

Bring the Children

1 "Bring the chil - dren un - to me," said Je - sus.
2 "Let the strong and let the weak," said Je - sus,
3 "One you love is soon to die," said Je - sus,
4 "Bring the chil - dren un - to me," said Je - sus.

"Bring them here for all to see," said Je - sus.
"come and hear the words I speak," said Je - sus.
"by the hands that cru - ci - fy," said Je - sus.
"Bring them here for all to see," said Je - sus.

"If you re - ceive them in my name, then
"If great you'd be then be the least— a
"But on the third day I will rise, and
"If you re - ceive them in my name, then

you re - ceive me just the same. 'Twas for the chil - dren
will - ing ser - vant at the feast and friend to chil - dren
strip a - way death's cruel dis - guise to look my chil - dren
you re - ceive me just the same. 'Twas for the chil - dren

that I came," said Je - sus.
such as these," said Je - sus.
in the eyes," said Je - sus.
that I came," said Je - sus.

Open the Door

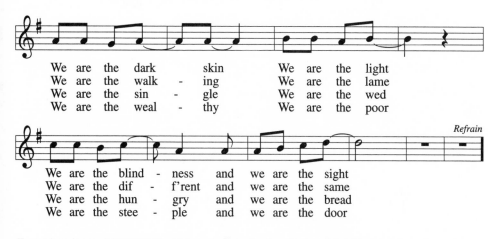

We are the dark skin / We are the light
We are the walk - ing / We are the lame
We are the sin - gle / We are the wed
We are the weal - thy / We are the poor

Refrain

We are the blind - ness and we are the sight
We are the dif - f'rent and we are the same
We are the hun - gry and we are the bread
We are the stee - ple and we are the door

76

How the Days Are Filled

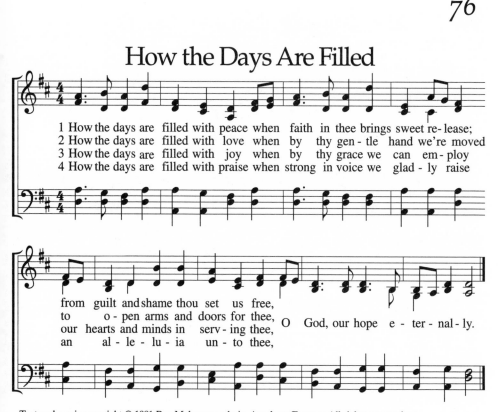

1 How the days are filled with peace when faith in thee brings sweet re-lease;
2 How the days are filled with love when by thy gen-tle hand we're moved
3 How the days are filled with joy when by thy grace we can em-ploy
4 How the days are filled with praise when strong in voice we glad-ly raise

from guilt and shame thou set us free,
to o-pen arms and doors for thee,   O God, our hope e-ter-nal-ly.
our hearts and minds in serv-ing thee,
an al-le-lu-ia un-to thee,

Many Colors, Many Kinds

Refrain

Man - y col - ors, man - y kinds, and ev - 'ry one of us is look - in' for some peace of mind—

Man - y col - ors, man - y kinds, and ev - 'ry one of us is look - in' for some peace of mind.

Last time to coda

1 When you're filled with wor - ry, feel - in' all a - lone, clos - in' in on trou - ble, far a - way from home— Just turn a - round, leave it all be - hind, for ev - 'ry one of us is look - in' for some peace of mind. *Refrain*

2 The Lord God ap - peared to poor Mar - y, called her bless - ed, spoke ten - der - ly, said "Bear my Son; please treat him kind"— for ev - 'ry one of us is look - in' for some peace of mind. *Refrain*

3 I walked in - to church, heard the preach-er say,

"Praise the Lord and pre-pare the way.

Now greet your neigh - bor and you're sure to find

Refrain

that ev-'ry one of us is look-in' for some peace of mind."

4 Yes, there's a need in ev-'ry-one

for blest as - sur - ance that the day will come

when the prom - ise be - comes the sign,

Refrain

and ev-'ry one of us will have a lit-tle peace of mind.

Coda

Ev - 'ry one of us is look-in' for some peace of mind.

Put On Love

1 Ho - ly, be - lov - ed, friends of God:

May peace be yours this day. May faith shine bright, may

hope fill the night all a - long your way.

Refrain

Put on love: It binds all things to-geth - er. Put on love in

per - fect u - ni - ty. Put on love: Wear it for each oth - er;

for each oth - er put on love.

2 Fill your cup with kind - ness.

Let pa - tience o - ver - flow. Like a stream of gen - tle

Refrain

ev - er - liv - ing wa - ter ev - 'ry - where you go.

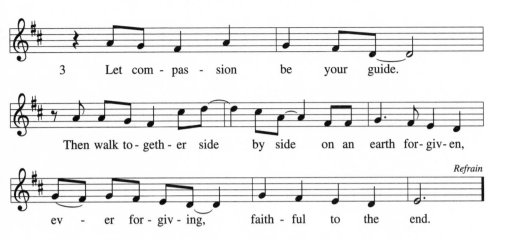

3 Let com - pas - sion be your guide.

Then walk to - geth - er side by side on an earth for - giv- en,

Refrain

ev - er for - giv - ing, faith - ful to the end.

79

God We Bless

Canon

1 God we bless, mer - ci - ful and in love with us.

2 And by grace we have been saved through faith, a gift in Christ.

3 Come to us, God of life, through your Ho - ly Spir - it.

4 Bring us peace this day, we are near and far a - way.

80

We Can Pray

Stanzas 1, 2

1 We can pray (we can pray) with our heads bowed right We can pray (we can
2 We can pray (we can pray) with our heads lift-ed high We can pray (we can

pray) with our hands fold-ed light We can pray (we can pray) with our
pray) with our hands to the sky We can pray (we can pray) with our

eyes shut tight For this is how God's peo-ple pray.
eyes o-pen wide For this is how God's peo-ple pray.

Refrain

Shh be qui-et We are pray - ing Shh be qui-et We are
Shout A - men We are pray - ing Shout A - men We are

pray - ing Shh be qui-et We are pray - ing For
Shout A - men

1 this is how God's peo-ple pray.

2 *To stanza 3* pray.

Instruments of Your Peace

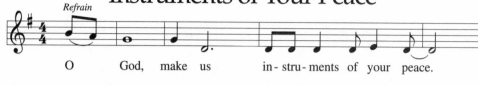

O God, make us in-stru-ments of your peace.

O God, take us, we are in-stru-ments of your peace.

1 Where there is ha-tred, let us sow love; where there is in-ju-ry, par-don;
2 Where there is dark-ness, let us be light; where there is sad-ness, be joy-ful;

where there is dis-cord, un-ion; and where there is doubt, sow faith.
where there's op-pres-sion, free-dom; and where there's de-spair, be hope.

3 For it is in giv-ing that we shall re-ceive, and it is in par-don-ing we're par-doned.

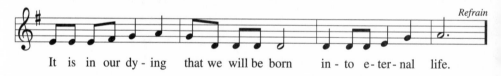

It is in our dy-ing that we will be born in-to e-ter-nal life.

Text: Prayer attributed to Francis of Assisi, adapt.
Text and music copyright © 1996 Ray Makeever, admin. Augsburg Fortress. All rights reserved.

O Loving God

Holy One, in You Alone

Refrain

We do not call this world our own, yet we will make this earth our
home; Ho-ly One, in you a-lone.

1 We do not claim this liv-ing word that we have
2 We do not claim this love of ours can tame the
3 We do not claim these seeds we sow will sprout and
4 We do not claim our prayers for change can re-ar-

heard is ours a-lone to give: We on-ly
pow'rs that lead our world to sin: We on-ly
grow from our own hope-ful hands: We on-ly
range this world by our own will: We on-ly

Refrain

know we have a heart in which it lives.
know we walk the road where Christ has been.
know we are the ground on which it lands.
know the ris-en Christ is with us still.

Text and music copyright © 1993 Ray Makeever, admin. Augsburg Fortress. All rights reserved.

We Come to the Hungry Feast

1 We come to the hun-gry feast hun-gry for the word of peace.
2 We come to the hun-gry feast hun-gry for a world re-leased
3 We come to the hun-gry feast hun-gry that the hun-ger cease,

To hun-gry hearts un-sat-is-fied the love of God is
from hun-gry peo-ple of ev-'ry kind, the poor in bod-y,
and know-ing, though we eat our fill, the hun-ger will stay

not de-nied. We come, we come to the hun-gry feast.
poor in mind. We come, we come to the hun-gry feast.
with us; still we come, we come to the hun-gry feast.

Even the Stones Will Cry Out

1 If the day should come when the hun-gry have no bread,
2 If the day should come when the scrip-tures are not read,
3 If the day should come when the air we breathe is dead,

when the rich have all been fed and .... still we can-not see;
when our lives are shaped in-stead by the im-ag-es of war;
when the whole earth has been bled till the earth will bleed no more;

when .. those who work for right are locked a-way, kept out of sight,
when all peo-ple far and near are slaves to greed and hate and fear,
when the o-ceans turn too warm, and o-ver-bear-ing sun brings harm,

and we're blind to what it means that we are free:
and we can't re-mem-ber what we're liv-ing for:
and the bar-ren land can bare-ly be re-stored:

Refrain

E-ven the stones will cry out for jus-tice;

e-ven the trees will sing out for peace.

The fire and wa-ter, the earth and sky,

all of cre-a-tion will cry out: Cry out!

1, 2
All of cre-a-tion will cry.

3
cry.

4 If the day should come when the crea-tures and the land

know us hand in hand in faith and hope and love; and

jus-tice leads to peace, and peace leads to in-teg-ri-ty, and cre-

a-tion is the home it's meant to be:

Final refrain

Then with the stones we'll cry out for jus-tice;

and with the trees we'll sing out for peace.

With fire and wa-ter, with earth and sky,

with all of cre-a - tion we'll cry out:

Cry out! With all of cre-a - tion we'll cry.

Blessed Are You

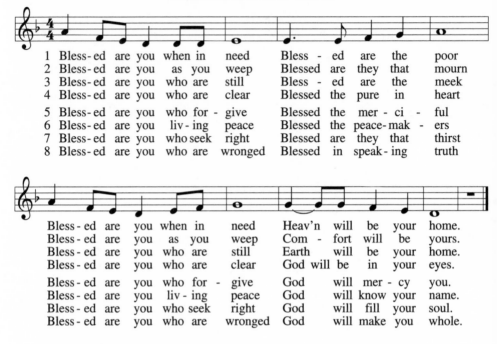

1 Bless-ed are you when in need / Bless-ed are the poor
2 Bless-ed are you as you weep / Blessed are they that mourn
3 Bless-ed are you who are still / Bless-ed are the meek
4 Bless-ed are you who are clear / Blessed the pure in heart

5 Bless-ed are you who for-give / Blessed the mer-ci-ful
6 Bless-ed are you liv-ing peace / Blessed the peace-mak-ers
7 Bless-ed are you who seek right / Blessed are they that thirst
8 Bless-ed are you who are wronged / Blessed in speak-ing truth

Bless-ed are you when in need / Heav'n will be your home.
Bless-ed are you as you weep / Com-fort will be yours.
Bless-ed are you who are still / Earth will be your home.
Bless-ed are you who are clear / God will be in your eyes.

Bless-ed are you who for-give / God will mer-cy you.
Bless-ed are you liv-ing peace / God will know your name.
Bless-ed are you who seek right / God will fill your soul.
Bless-ed are you who are wronged / God will make you whole.

On Earth As in Heaven

Refrain

On earth as in heav-en, let the will of God be done.

On earth as in heav-en, let there al - ways be a

ris - ing sun, and let it rise on ev - 'ry - one.

1 Let the air we breathe be Spir - it now— Here on
2 Let .... jus - tice be the path we walk— Here on
3 Let our si - lent tears in hope a - bound— Here on
4 Let the sound of laugh - ter fill the air— Here on

earth as in heav - en. Let the words we speak be
earth as in heav - en. Let .... love of life be
earth as in heav - en. Let the dance we dance bless
earth as in heav - en. Let the song we sing go

Refrain

truth some - how— Here on earth as in heav - en.
more than talk— Here on earth as in heav - en.
ho - ly ground— Here on earth as in heav - en.
ev - 'ry - where— Here on earth as in heav - en.

Jubilee!

1 Give us faith to let our lands lie fal-low, then to rest our hands—that
2 Give us meek-ness to con-fess when fail-ure binds us to dis - tress; then
3 Give us cour-age, ho - ly vi - sion in our hearts to see the pris - on,
4 Give us wis - dom to dis-cern the truth be-yond what we have earned; that
5 Give us joy a - mid the sor - row, ris-ing from the dust in dance. We

push and pull and work for gain—to hal-low once a - gain thy name.
move our wor-ried tongues to speak: May we be-come the love we seek.
be the cap-tive now set free from ston - y mind and hate and greed.
what be-longed to each at birth may be re-turned as seed to earth.
sing to - day and shape to-mor - row: Jus-tice gives us all a chance.

Refrain

Ju - bi - lee! Ju - bi - lee! Come, O God of grace, take the

place of hon-or at the ju - bi-lee. Ju - bi - lee! Ju - bi - lee! Come,O

God of grace, take the place of hon-or at the ju-bi-lee.

It Won't Be Long

1 It won't be long now it won't be long
2 Sis - ters be strong now sis - ters be strong
3 Broth - ers be strong now broth - ers be strong
4 Free - dom our song now free - dom our song

It won't be long now it won't be long till
Sis - ters be strong now sis - ters be strong till
Broth - ers be strong now broth - ers be strong till
Free - dom our song now free - dom our song till

jus - tice comes roll-ing like a might-y stream
jus - tice comes roll-ing like a might-y stream
jus - tice comes roll-ing like a might-y stream
jus - tice comes roll-ing like a might-y stream

It won't be long now it won't be long.
It won't be long now it won't be long.
It won't be long now it won't be long.
It won't be long now it won't be long.

*May be sung in canon

90

Let Peace Fill the Earth

1 Let peace fill the earth as the wa - ters fill the sea.
2 Let peace fill the earth as the moun - tains fill the sky.
3 Let peace fill the earth as the light that fill the fire.
4 Let peace fill the earth as the hope that fills our song.

Let love and jus - tice flow like a might - y rush - ing stream.
Let love and jus - tice flow like the wing - ed birds that fly.
Let love and jus - tice flow like the friend - ship we de - sire.
Let love and jus - tice flow like the voic - es sing - ing a - long.

And may we see the day when war and blood - shed cease,
And may we see the day when war and blood - shed cease,
And may we see the day when war and blood - shed cease,
And may we see the day when war and blood - shed cease,

and through - out all the world there will be peace.
and through - out all the world there will be peace.
and through - out all the world there will be peace.
and through - out all the world there will be peace.

Write Your Law upon Our Hearts

Refrain

Write your law up-on our hearts, O God; we are your peo - ple.

Write your law up-on our hearts, O God. 1 "Be -

hold the days are com - ing," says our God (who can fore-tell),
2 "I will make a cov - e - nant, not like the one of old,
3 "I will make a cov - e - nant and this is where I'll start:
4 "I will make a cov - e - nant and ev - 'ry - one shall know:

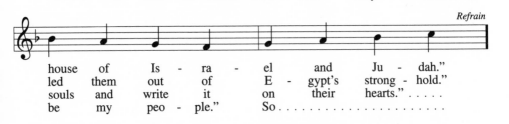

"When I will make a cov - e - nant with the
when I took my peo - ple by the hand and I
.... I will put my law with - in their ....
.... I will be their God and they shall ....

Refrain

house of Is - ra - el and Ju - dah."
led them out of E - gypt's strong - hold."
souls and write it on their hearts." .....
be my peo - ple." So ....

We Will Serve God

Refrain

We will serve God in all that we do,
all that we say, all a-long the way. We will
serve God, whose sto-ry we will tell:

Last time to coda

We will serve the God of Is - ra - el.

1 We will serve the God who brought us out of E - gypt's land, who
2 We will serve the God who came in Je - sus Christ, our friend, who
3 We will serve the God who made us, formed us from the clay, who

kept us all in safe - ty, who took us by the hand; who
lived a - mong the peo - ple, who loved them to the end; who
breathes in - to our bod - ies, who breathes in - to each day; who

fed us in the des - ert, who met us on the shore, who
went in - to the des - ert, who taught up - on the shore, who
feeds us in the des - ert, who meets us on the shore, who

Refrain

led us through the wa - ter, who's with us ev - er - more.
walked a - cross the wa - ter, who's with us ev - er - more.
leads us through the wa - ter, who's with us ev - er - more.

Coda

el, we will serve the God of Is - ra - el.

Around the Great Commandment

Love the Lord your God with all your heart, and your neigh-bor as your-self.

Love the Lord your God with all your heart, and your neigh-bor as your-self. Love the

Lord, love the Lord, love the Lord your God. Love the

Lord, love the Lord, love the Lord your God.

Love your neigh-bor as you love your-self; God is lov - ing you.

Love your neigh-bor as you love your-self; God is lov - ing you. This is the

great and first com-mand-ment and the sec - ond, too. This is the

great and first com-mand-ment and the sec - ond, too.

This canon may be sung in two ways:
• Part 1 only, with voices entering at each measure (2, 3, or 4 parts)
• As a whole, with voices entering at the numbers (2, 3, or 4 parts)

Someone in Need of Your Love

Refrain

some-one in need of your love: Some-one who's

lone - ly, lost on their way. Sigh-in' or cry - in',

may - be near dy- in', some - one who can't find the right words to

say: There's some-one in need of your love.

3 Well, it could be the strang-er stretched out on the

road as you're tra - velin' to Jer - i - cho. Or it

could be some - bod - y much clos - er to home,

Refrain

some - one you al - read - y know. There's

With All Your Heart

Refrain

With all your heart, with all your mind, with all your spir-it—

With all your heart, with all your mind, with ev-'ry fi - ber in your soul—

With all your heart, with all your mind, with ev-'ry-thing that makes you whole—

Love your God, your-self, and your neigh-bor with your heart and mind and soul.

1 "Tell us, Je - sus" (Tell us Je - sus) came and said the Phar - i - sees.

"Tell us, Je - sus" (Tell us Je - sus) "Which law is the great-est, please?"

"Tell us, Je - sus" (Tell us Je - sus) "which com-mand-ment to o - bey—

Refrain

which one stands a - bove the oth - ers?" Je - sus then was heard to say:

2 Je - sus told them (Je - sus told them) as he took their test in hand,

Je - sus told them (Je - sus told them) "Lov-ing God's the great com-mand."

Je - sus told them (Je - sus told them) "There's a sec-ond like un - to:

Love your neigh - bor as you'd love that lov - ing

Refrain

self that's a part of you."

Give It Away

1 Have you heard the sto - ry 'bout the rich man

Give it a - way,   **give it a - way**   Who asked Je - sus how to

get to the prom-ised land **Give it a - way,**   **give it a - way**   He had

kept all the com-mand-ments ev- 'ry one   **Give it a - way,**

give it a - way   There was just one thing that

he had nev - er done **Give it a - way,**   **give it a - way.**

Refrain

Go,   **sell what you have,**   **sell what you have**   **and**

give it a - way   **to the poor.**   **Sell what you have,**

To stanzas

then come and fol - low me.

End

Then come and fol - low me.

2 When the rich man heard the words that Je-sus said **Give it a-way,**

give it a-way He walked a-way sad-ly shak-ing his head **Give it a-way,**

give it a-way For though his walk was straight and his path was sure

Give it a-way, give it a-way When he passed the gate he

Refrain
would not touch the poor **Give it a-way, give it a-way.**

3 Have you heard the one a-bout the cam-el **Give it a-way,**

give it a-way who tried to squeeze through the eye of a nee-dle

Give it a-way, give it a-way Yes, it's hard to get the heav-y-

lad-en through **Give it a-way, give it a-way** So light-en up your load and

Refrain
see what God can do **Give it a-way, give it a-way.**

Tell What God Has Done for Us

Refrain

Come, all you faith-ful, swell the cho-rus, sing the song for a - ges sung. Hand in hand in a thou-sand tongues, we will tell what God has done for us.

1 Tell how God made earth and sky, wa - ter low and fire .... high;
2 Tell how God called Ab - ra - ham, told him 'bout the prom-ised land.
3 Tell how God set Is - rael free, led them through the rag - ing sea,
4 Tell how God took hu - man form: Je - sus Christ, of Mar - y born;
5 Tell how God lives on to - day in the love that lights our way;

Refrain

swim - ming, walk-ing, fly - ing things, des - ert sands and bub-bling springs.
Tell how Sa - rah laughed, gave birth, turn - ing doubt to ho - ly mirth.
fed them man - na from a - bove, then gave them the law in love.
mak - ing flesh the cov - e - nant, grace and truth from heav - en sent.
spark - ing joy and calm - ing fear, breath - ing life when death is near.

Keep the Faith

Fight the good fight, fin-ish the race, keep the faith.

Fight the good fight, fin-ish the race, keep the faith.

1 God is be-fore you, God is be-hind you,
2 God will help you start, give you the right part,

God is a-bove and be-low.
God will be there to be-friend.

God is be-side you, God is with-in you,
God will up-hold you, ev-er en-fold you,

God is wher-ev-er you go.
God will be there at the end.

Living Thanksgiving

1 There is no song with-out the sing - ing
2 There is no love with-out re - ceiv - ing
3 There is no risk with-out the tak - ing
4 There is no song with-out the sing - ing

There is no gift with-out the bring - ing
There is no hope with-out be - liev - ing
There is no change with-out the break - ing
There is no gift with-out the bring - ing

There is no life with-out the liv - ing
There is no faith with-out the leav - ing
There is no heart with-out the ach - ing
There is no life with-out the liv - ing

Last time to coda

And no thanks with-out the giv - ing
No heal - ing with-out the grieving
And no soul with-out the wak-ing
And no thanks with-out the giv - ing

Coda

Giv - ing   Liv - ing   Giv - ing:

Liv - ing thanks - giv - ing   Giv- ing

Liv- ing   Giv- ing: Liv- ing thanks- giv - ing

When You Call

When you call, O God, I will an - swer.

When you call, O God, I will come.

When you call, O God, I will fol - low you.

Show me the way, lead me home.

Comes a New Song

From ev - 'ry tribe and ev - 'ry na - tion,

from ev - 'ry peo - ple and ev - 'ry tongue,

from ev - 'ry cor - ner of the whole cre - a - tion

comes a new song that must be sung.

Death Be Never Last

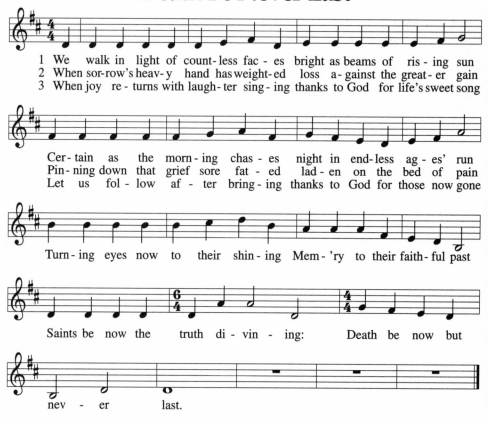

1 We walk in light of count-less fac - es bright as beams of ris - ing sun
2 When sor-row's heav-y hand has weight-ed loss a-gainst the great-er gain
3 When joy re - turns with laugh-ter sing-ing thanks to God for life's sweet song

Cer-tain as the morn-ing chas - es night in end-less ag - es' run
Pin-ning down that grief sore fat - ed lad-en on the bed of pain
Let us fol-low af - ter bring-ing thanks to God for those now gone

Turn-ing eyes now to their shin-ing Mem- 'ry to their faith-ful past

Saints be now the truth di - vin - ing: Death be now but

nev - er last.

Text and music copyright © 1993 Ray Makeever, admin. Augsburg Fortress. All rights reserved.

Between the Times

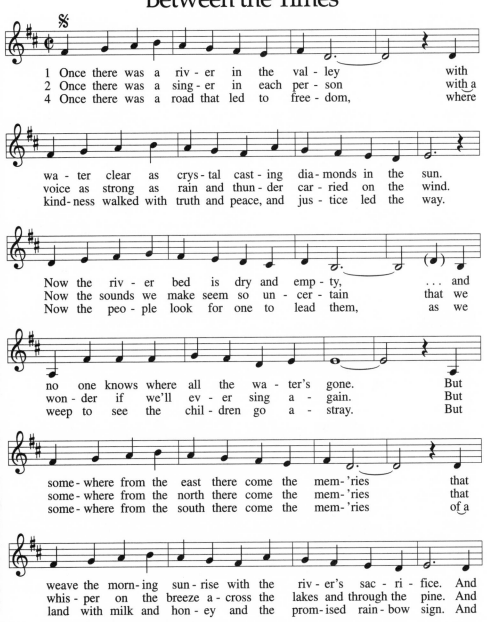

1 Once there was a riv - er in the val - ley with
2 Once there was a sing - er in each per - son with a
4 Once there was a road that led to free - dom, where

wa - ter clear as crys - tal cast - ing dia - monds in the sun.
voice as strong as rain and thun - der car - ried on the wind.
kind - ness walked with truth and peace, and jus - tice led the way.

Now the riv - er bed is dry and emp - ty, . . . and
Now the sounds we make seem so un - cer - tain that we
Now the peo - ple look for one to lead them, as we

no one knows where all the wa - ter's gone. But
won - der if we'll ev - er sing a - gain. But
weep to see the chil - dren go a - stray. But

some - where from the east there come the mem - 'ries that
some - where from the north there come the mem - 'ries that
some - where from the south there come the mem - 'ries of a

weave the morn - ing sun - rise with the riv - er's sac - ri - fice. And
whis - per on the breeze a - cross the lakes and through the pine. And
land with milk and hon - ey and the prom - ised rain - bow sign. And

Song continues on next page ▶

those who trust the   move-ment of the   cen - turies   can still
those who trust the   move-ment of the   cen - turies   can still
those who trust the   move-ment of the   cen - turies   can still

see   the   riv - er   flow   be - tween   the   times.
hear   a   song   to   sing   be - tween   the   times.
walk a - long   the   road   be - tween   the   times.

Refrain

Be - tween   the   times   of   plen - ty,

(1) when the
(2) when the
(4) when . . . . .

wa - ter's   just   a   trick - le   in   our   lives,
song is   just   a   whis - per   in   our   lives,
free - dom   is   im - pris - oned   in   our   lives,

at   the

time   that   we   must   grieve   be - cause the   words that we   be -

Last time to coda

lieve aren't com-ing   true: What shall we   do   be - tween the

To stanza 2   *D.S.*   *To stanza 3*

times?   times?

3 We will look to the west and be-hold the ho-ly moun-tain:

home to the spir-it of all peo-ple gone be-fore. We will

put to the test the faith that we can

count on, all the strength and all the wis-dom, all the

hope and all the vi-sion, all the beau-ty that still

To stanza 4 D.S.

lives in them who bid us walk this way once more.

Coda

times? What shall we do be-tween the times?

For to This End

Scriptural Index

Genesis
1   In the water, 68
1:1-5   Walk across the water, 69
7-9   In the water, 68
12:1-2   I will make you into a great nation, 57

Exodus
14-15   Walk across the water, 69

Leviticus
25-27   Jubilee! 88

1 Samuel
3:1-10   When you call, 100

Psalms
8   Who are we, 33
34   I will bless you, O God, 34
51   Be merciful, O God, 35
51:16   Rise up and sing! 7
61   Hear my cry, O God, 36
62   Rest in God alone, 37
67   Let all the people praise, 38
80   Behold and tend this vine, 39
85   Dancing at the harvest, 40
95   Oh, come, let us worship, 5
100   Come with joy, 41
100   Jubilate, 14
100   Make a joyful noise, 4
103   Bless the Lord, 42
104   When you send forth your Spirit, 43
105   Tell what God has done for us, 97
118:25, 26   Holy, holy, 22
118:25, 26   Holy, holy, holy Lord, 21
128   Bless us, O God, 44
130:5-8   Bright and Morning Star, 50
143   Show me the way, 45
145   God is compassionate, 46
146   Sing unto the Lord, 47
148   Praise and exalt God, 48

Isaiah
2:1-5   Let peace fill the earth, 90
6:3   Holy, holy, 22
6:3   Holy, holy, holy Lord, 21
9:5   Let peace fill the earth, 90
25:6   This is the feast, 12

Jeremiah
31:31-34   Write your law upon our hearts, 91

Joel
2:28   In the last days, 70

Amos
5:24   It won't be long, 89
5:24   Let peace fill the earth, 90

Matthew
2:13-23   Holy Child, 54
5:1-12   Blessed are you, 86
5:13-16   Brighter than the sun, 64
6:10   On earth as in heaven, 87
11:28   In the water, 68
11:28-30   Come unto me, 26
14:22-33   Walk across the water, 69
16:24-26   Thanksgiving to the living God, 3
21:1-11   Hosanna! Come and deliver, 59
21:28-32   There was the Word, 55
22:34-40   With all your heart, 95
22:37-39   Around the great commandment, 93

Mark
9:30-37   Bring the children, 74
10:17-25   Give it away, 96
12:30-31   Around the great commandment, 93

Luke
1:67-79   Blessed are you, Lord, 49
2:14   Gloria in excelsis Deo, 13
6:20-23   Blessed are you, 86
10:25-37   Someone in need of your love, 94
18:18-30   Spirit of the living God, 72
19:40   Even the stones will cry out, 85
22:14-19   Come and dine at the table, 27
23:32-43   Jesus, remember me, 60
23:32-43   Strange King, 61

John
1:1-14   There was the Word, 55
1:16   From the fullness of God, 18

1:29	Lamb of God, 23, 24
1:29	Lamb of God, come take away, 25
1:29-42	Come and see, 56
2:1-10	Just as Jesus told us, 29
3:1-8	Baby born again, 67
4:5-30	All was not well, 58
4:13	In the water, 68
4:24	In spirit and truth, 73
13:1-17	Take off your shoes, 62
20:1-10	Good news, alleluia! 65

Acts

2:17-18	In the last days, 70
2:21	Everyone who calls upon the name, 17
2:33	Fill us with your Spirit, 71

Romans

8:1-16	Thanksgiving to the living God, 3
12:1-2	Holy One, in you alone, 83
14:7-10	For to this end, 104
15:7	Come, let us worship God, 2
15:7	People of the Word, 1

1 Corinthians

10:16-17	This bread that we break, 30
15:20	Christ has been raised, 66

2 Corinthians

5:1-20	Awake, O sleeper! 63
5:17	Brighter than the sun, 64

Ephesians

2:8	God we bless, 79

Colossians

3:12-17	Put on love, 78

2 Timothy

4:7	Keep the faith, 98

2 Peter

1:19	Bright and Morning Star, 50

Revelation

5:9-13	This is the feast, 12
7:9-10	Comes a new song, 101
15:3-4	This is the feast, 12
22:16	Bright and Morning Star, 50